INDIAN REFORM ASSOCIATION.

WHY THE INDIANS ARE GRATEFUL TO LORD RIPON.

BY

V. M. SAMARTH, B.A., M.R.A.S.

38, PARLIAMENT STREET, LONDON, S.W.

1885.

In the interest of creating a more extensive selection of rare historical book reprints, we have chosen to reproduce this title even though it may possibly have occasional imperfections such as missing and blurred pages, missing text, poor pictures, markings, dark backgrounds and other reproduction issues beyond our control. Because this work is culturally important, we have made it available as a part of our commitment to protecting, preserving and promoting the world's literature. Thank you for your understanding.

INDIAN REFORM ASSOCIATION.

The INDIAN REFORM ASSOCIATION exists with the object of informing the British public of all facts relating to the condition and desires of the people of India, so far as they can be ascertained from the best sources; to collect and diffuse accurate information in such a form as shall be intelligible to persons not acquainted with the technicalities of Indian life and administration, through the Press, public meetings, conferences, and other means calculated to influence Parliament and the Executive, so that increased attention may be given, by both, to the welfare and progress of the Indian people.

38, PARLIAMENT STREET, LONDON, S.W.

WHY THE INDIANS ARE GRATEFUL TO LORD RIPON.

Lord Ripon's retirement has agitated the whole of India. His popularity with natives of all classes, educated as well as uneducated, has been great—almost unprecedented. The great demonstrations of genuine admiration of which one has been hearing for the last few months leave no doubt in this respect. What is the cause of this enthusiasm? This is rather a difficult question to answer—difficult inasmuch as Indian society is such a complex mass, and a variety of motives, oftentimes antagonistic to each other, get mixed up in an inexplicable manner; and the wonder is that all classes of such a community should have joined with one voice in the expression of their sincere admiration of Lord Ripon. I will try to explain, as briefly as I can, the causes of this enthusiasm. Let us transport ourselves to the times of a quarter of a century ago—the time of what is called the Indian Mutiny of 1857. The effects of Lord Dalhousie's administration were becoming every day clearer to the natives of India. Many native kingdoms had disappeared into the ever-increasing vortex of British conquest, and with them had vanished all avenues to power, and scope for native ability and ambition. The people, therefore, looked with dismay at these unwelcome changes. They were puzzled, and did not know where they were drifting. Now the Sepoy Mutiny broke out. The people—I mean the people taken as a whole—did not join it; but they were interested spectators. Would lost opportunities return? Would they regain their independence? These were thoughts which, I have no doubt, were exercising them. It was mainly a revolt of the Sepoys—the native soldiery in the pay of the British. The Mutiny was suppressed, the Sepoy was defeated, by the unexampled bravery of English soldiers. But what proportions would the Mutiny have assumed if the people had joined in it? The wisdom of English statesmanship was nowhere better displayed than in the quick perception of this fact. The policy of conciliation prevailed over that of revenge. The Mutiny brought the greedy reign of John Company to an inglorious end. The Crown of England assumed the direct administration of India, and the memorable proclamation by the Queen to the "Princes and People" of India was issued to Her Majesty's expectant Indian subjects. This proclamation—which has since come to be regarded as the Magna Charta of Indian liberties—promised justice and political equality to the natives of India, without distinction of race or creed, as between themselves and between their British-born fellow-subjects; and, among other things, it promised to admit natives to positions of trust and responsibility. These pledges from the Sovereign of Great Britain and Ireland were accepted as sufficient, and India from the foot of the Himalayas to Cape Kamorin was content to enter on the new state of things. Successive Viceroys have repeated these pledges on the part of their gracious Sovereign; but very little willingness is evinced to act on them. The blessings of Western culture are making the people to feel that, in spite of repeated verbal assurances, very little is done to raise their political status; and that, worse still, whenever a well-meaning Viceroy attempts to do anything in that direction his hands are tied by the European official and non-official classes in India, who invariably exhibit extreme unwillingness to rise superior to motives of personal aggrandisement; that, in fact, this class of Europeans has always stood between themselves and any concession of political power. I have been rather diffuse, I am afraid; but my endeavour is to show what kind of feeling underlies almost all native agitations and demonstrations. The natives feel themselves wronged when they find the fulfilment of the pledges given by the Queen of England withheld from them. Nobody is so unwise as to expect England to withdraw herself from the country. No, not yet; not for a long time to come. There is a limit which prudence imposes on even the most absurd expectations.

Here, then, is the key to the demonstrations in favour of Lord Ripon. To understand them well, I must again ask the reader to let me state here in brief the circumstances which had immediately preceded Lord Ripon's advent to India. A beginning was made in the able Viceroyalty of Lord Mayo to *educate* natives—as they say—in the management of municipal affairs, by admitting the municipalities of certain large towns to a small share of independence in matters of expenditure; and it was intended to make a further concession in this direction in the event of this experiment proving favourable. Unfortunately, however, Lord Mayo met a premature death at the hands of an assassin amidst the sincre regrets of all natives. Lord Northbrook succeeded him. He encouraged his predecessor's municipal policy; but he gave a rude shock to the susceptibilities of natives by his highhanded action in the case of a great Hindoo prince. Lord Lytton's whole reign was one of imperialism and highhandedness. He began rather well. His treatment of the so-called Fuller case was approved and applauded by natives. One Fuller had assaulted a native under circumstances in no way excusable. He was tried before the ordinary court of justice, and let off on some flimsy excuse. The case was unfavourably commented on in the native press. The outcry was great. Such cases of assault on natives had become rather frequent, and in almost every case the European offender managed to escape the law. The feeling was steadily gaining ground in the native mind that there was no justice to be had as against a European; and the Queen's pledge of equal treatment to natives and Europeans alike was every day losing its force with natives. Lord Lytton reviewed the case in an able memorandum, and dealt justice. This had a reassuring effect on the native mind. This was almost the only oasis in the wilderness of Lord Lytton's administration. His other measures were described by natives, as well as by Europeans, in the most uncomplimentary epithets I have ever heard. In the beginning of 1877, he was revelling in the gorgeous display of imperialistic pageantry in connection with the assumption of the title of Empress by the Queen, when hundreds of thousands of India's inhabitants were perishing of hunger. Sir R. Temple, to whom the management of the famine relief was entrusted, was indulging in his pet ideas when people were dying like so many flies. The famine was used as an excuse for the imposition of an iniquitous tax, and the funds realised from this tax were appropriated—or rather, misappropriated—towards the Afghan War, which was universally regarded as an unjust war; and when all these doings were rather severely criticised in the vernacular press, an Act was passed to stifle free discussion. This Act is still remembered in India as the Gagging Act. In short, the whole administration of India under Lord Lytton consisted of a series of high-handed acts, and boastful, unsubstantial talk. The old days of imperialism were revived with a vengeance; so that, when Lord Ripon arrived, he was received with a full heart by the people as a messenger of peace and justice.

The very first words of Lord Ripon were calculated to allay the public mind. The phantom of imperialism was chased away. "Deeds; not words." Lord Ripon in his very first speech, at which I had the honour of being present, asked to be judged by his actions, and not to expect any very high sounding phrases from him; and the people were promised peace and progress. He proceeded to carry out this programme in a systematic way. The odious vernacular Press Act was abolished. Afghanistan was pacified, although the injustice done to Shere Ali, its former ruler, was past remedy. The Native States, which were slightly alarmed since the high-handedness displayed towards one of them by Lord Northbrook, and the assumption of the Imperial title by the Queen in Lord Lytton's time, were assured that the British Government would respect and abide by its treaty engagements with them. Thus peace, having been restored, the vessel of state was steered towards progress. Encouragement was given, however slight, to local industry and local manufactures by requesting the subordinate governments to purchase articles made in India for use in offices. The local self-government policy of Lord Mayo was given a distinct recognition and stimulus, and the elective principle was introduced and insisted upon where the people were ripe for such a step, but were kept down by the love of power of the local magistrates, who, of course, did not like the Viceroy's views. But the crowning piece of his administration was what is popularly called the Ilbert Bill. This has a history about it. In the course of business the Act for the criminal administration of India—the Criminal Procedure Act, as it is called—came for revision before the Viceroy and his Council. The Act contains certain sections exempting Europeans and Americans from being tried by native magistrates, under certain circumstances. One of the native members of the Viceroy's Legislative Council asked the Viceroy whether it was thought to ever remove this blot on native character, and was promised that the request would be considered separately. As a sort of result of this request, after due consideration, an amendment was drafted and introduced into the Legislative Council by the Hon. Mr. Ilbert to the above Act, empowering native magistrates, of a certain standing and under very strict conditions, to try European criminals. Upon this, a howl was raised by the European community in India, and all sorts of things were said about Lord Ripon. What followed is too well known. The Act was passed after a great deal of clipping and cutting, till it altogether changed its form and shape. But the natives like Lord Ripon for the courage of his convictions, and as one who tried to bestow on them some concession in the direction of the Royal proclamation of 1858. The demonstrations in favour of Lord Ripon are demonstrations in favour of the policy he pursued, which is the policy dictated by the Queen and the Parliament of England as the only one which is consistent with their mission in India.

INDIAN REFORM ASSOCIATION.

President:

Vice-Presidents:

ARTHUR ARNOLD, M.P.
WILFRID SCAWEN BLUNT.
GENERAL SIR WM. COGHLAN, R.A., K.C.B.
MAJOR-GENERAL CRIPPS.
JAMES CROPPER, M.P.
SIR R. H. DAVIES, K.C.S.I., late Lieut.-Governor of the Punjaub.
J. F. B. FIRTH, M.P.
THOMAS HUGHES, Q.C.
MAJOR-GENERAL HARRISON, late of Bengal Army.
MAJOR-GENERAL HILL, Bengal Staff Corps.
JUSTIN MCCARTHY, M.P.
JUSTIN H. MCCARTHY, M.P.
SIR CHRISTOPHER RAWLINSON, late Chief Justice, Madras.
R. T. REID, M.P., Q.C.
J. E. THOROLD ROGERS, M.P.
MOHAMED ALI ROGAY, late Member of Legislative Council, Bombay.
JOHN SLAGG, M.P.
WILLIAM SUMMERS, M.P.
SIR R. K. WILSON, Bart.
WILLIAM WOODALL, M.P.
MAJOR-GENERAL RALPH YOUNG, late R.E.

General Committee:

William Clarke.	E. J. W. Gibb.
C. D. Collet.	Sidney Goult.
Godfrey Collins.	N. B. Gundevia.
William Coghlan.	J. Seymour Keay.
Richard Congreve, LL.D.	John Noble.
J. S. Cotton, M.A.	Colonel R. Osborne.
R. Needham Cust, late Bengal Civil Service.	F. H. Plumptre.
	Colonel M. Ramsay.
E. N. Dillon, M.A., LL.D.	George Sibley, C.E., C.I.E.
J. E. Elles.	T. G. Southerst.
H. G. Fordham.	A. G. Symonds, M.A.
J. J. Gazdar.	Major De Winton.
N. L. Ghosh.	

Executive Committee:

G. B. Clark, M.D., Chairman.	A. H. Haggard, late of Bengal Civil Service.
W. C. Borlase, M.P.	Hamid Ali.
Major Evans Bell.	N. J. Moolla.
M. M. Bhownagari.	Parkinson Oates, M.D.
J. N. Banerjee.	Hodgson Pratt.
William Digby, C.I.E.	J. Rowlands.
T. W. Rhys Davids.	Rajah Rampal Singh.
	W. Martin Wood.

GEORGE FOGGO, *Secretary.*
A. K. SETTNA, *Corresponding Secretary for India.*

THE COSSACK AT THE GATE OF INDIA.

BY

LIEUT.-GENERAL CHARLES LIONEL SHOWERS,

BENGAL STAFF CORPS;

LATE POLITICAL RESIDENT IN RAJPUTANA AND CENTRAL INDIA.

DEDICATED TO THE ELECTORS OF THE UNITED KINGDOM—
PRESENT AND COMING.

London:
SIMPKIN, MARSHALL & Co.,
STATIONERS' HALL COURT, E.C.

Price Sixpence.

TO THE

ELECTORS OF THE UNITED KINGDOM—PRESENT AND COMING.

In the full and confident belief that the newly-enfranchised electors will recognise their solemn and responsible duty by returning Members to Parliament who will support, impartially, only such leaders as will uphold the honour and interest of Great Britain abroad, and provide for the people at home, I desire to dedicate to them the following leaves—veritable "Sibylline Leaves" they will be found, I venture to affirm—in respect of the risk of impending war with Russia, in defence of our Indian Empire, which has been entailed by persistent neglect of my repeated warnings.

Now, with Russia at our gate, the policy which I have consistently advocated to check her advance will at length, I hope, command attention. Though late in the day, it is one which, if even now adopted thoroughly, consistently, as a steadfast national policy, as distinguished from party oscillations and reversals, may yet avail, I venture to think, to retrieve time wasted, ground lost, confidence shaken.

March, 1885.

"We can govern India,' wrote Froude, "we cannot govern Ireland."* Why? Because in India officers are appointed to the several posts under the Government according to their proved capacity and fitness for the same respectively. Whereas in England, at every party change, straightway is installed a Ministry of the Heaven-born INEVITABLES. Poor John Bull, like his venerable prototype, Sinbad the sailor, is forthwith saddled with the "old man of the sea," in the person of inevitable Secretaries of State in every department, and equally ungetriddable. Not a word in the English language—nothing, in short, but a phrase specially coined for the occasion could adequately designate the incubus with which the nation is afflicted under the present system of virtually irresponsible Privilege.

I will first detail the policy I advocated in a State Paper, printed for official and private circulation so far back as 1869, for the securing of the North-West frontier of India, when as yet Russia was far distant; and next, the course which I submitted for the consideration of Her Majesty's Government in July, 1882, with respect to Egypt, our highway to India. Both, I venture to affirm, will be seen, with reference to succeeding events as a foil, to have been equally sound. My voice has been that of one "crying in the wilderness," because calculated to disturb the complacent optimism of selfish "last-our-time" politicians successively in power.

With respect to the first subject, I would add that as each succeeding stage of the Central Asian Question served to verify and accentuate my views by the foil of the reverse, I have consistently advocated their adoption from time to

---

* English in Ireland. Vol. III., p. 584.

time,* even up to July last (1884), when impressed with the impolicy of the Lumsden Mission, inasmuch as constituting a virtual condoning of the annexation of Merv, I wrote a Paper with a view of stopping its dispatch, and suggesting a course of action instead, calculated, in my humble judgment, practically to neutralise the injurious effects of that faithless measure. All in vain. The Mission was dispatched, and Russia, under the mask of accepting our Foreign Office proposal for a Joint Commission for the delimitation of the frontier, utilized the interval in seizing strategic posts within the territorial scope of the Commission. Hence the present crisis.

Before submitting, however, my view of the measures necessary for dealing with the situation, let us first consider the claim of the Government, as demanded by the Prime Minister and his subordinates in their places last night (5th inst.) to be left unquestioned to deal with it. This will necessitate a brief review of their past negotiations with the Russian Government as exhibited in recent Central Asia Blue Books and Parliamentary debates.

Turning first to the Central Asia Blue Book No. 1, 1884, it will be observed that the first dispatch of that correspondence is a telegram from Earl Granville to Mr. Thomson, British Minister at Teheran, dated the 30th Dec., 1881, inquiring " with reference to reports which had appeared in the newspapers in England that the Turkomans at Merv had surrendered to the Russians, whether any intelligence had reached him to that effect ? " The answer in the negative

---

* " The Central Asian Question," by Colonel Charles Lionel Showers, late Political Resident in Rajputana and Central India. Henry S. King and Co., 1873. Second Edition, Mitchell and Co., Charing Cross, 1879.

then returned by Mr. Thomson was reiterated by him to a similar inquiry repeated by Earl Granville on the 9th February, 1884—two years and two months afterwards—on the authority of the *St. Petersburg Gazette.* Mr. Thomson's answer is so unqualified that, being short, it may be given *in extenso* :—" *Teheran,* Feb. 10, 1884, 4.24 p.m. I have no confirmation of reported submission of Merv Chiefs. Intelligence just received, dated 3rd February, states that Chiefs had rejected Russian demand for submission." Five days later—viz., on the 15th February, Sir E. Thornton, our Ambassador at St. Petersburg, telegraphs to Earl Granville that, "His Imperial Majesty had determined to accept the allegiance which the representatives of the Merv Turkomans had sworn at Askabad, and to send an officer to administer the government of that region." This dispatch but too fittingly closes the correspondence—the disastrous event announced therein being but a foregone conclusion in view of the uniform yielding to unwarrantable Russian demands on the part of the British Foreign Office, marking its whole course. So early in the negotiations, indeed, as March, 1882, the key-note of the surrender was sounded in Earl Granville's dispatch, dated 22nd March, 1882, to the address of Sir E. Thornton, British Ambassador at St. Petersburgh (No. 18 of the correspondence), practically yielding, while demurring to its principle, the demand of the Russian Ambassador "that the delimitation of the Russo-Persian frontier was a matter which concerned Russia and the Shah exclusively." The concluding words of that memorable dispatch are as follows: "But I continued that, without giving up that principle, we should be satisfied if an agreement were arrived at between Russia and Persia in the sense of Lord Hartington's proposal *without England being a party to it.*" (The italics are mine). Persia being thus deserted by England, and left to cope alone and unsupported with the overwhelming power of Russia, British interests in this momentous question were thereby equally abandoned. The subsequent annexation of Merv by Russia, as well as further aggressions on Persian territory, was, I can only repeat, a foregone conclusion.

Let us turn next to the debate in the House of Lords, on the 11th March, 1884, on Lord Lytton's motion.

In reviewing the controversy between Lord Salisbury and Lord Granville, I trust I need hardly disclaim all thought of importing a shade of party feeling into a momentous matter which concerns in common all parties and interests in the United Kingdom. Holding, however, with Bishop Warburton that, "Orthodoxy is my doxy; heterodoxy anyone else's doxy that differs from my own," I am bound to give my humble voice in favour of Lord Salisbury's position in regard to the feeling of the people of India about the advance of Russia, since in my Paper of 1869 it will be found (pp. 10-11) how strongly I insisted on this being a vital element in framing our North-West Frontier policy—the same warning being reiterated in my further published Papers of 1873 and 1879. His Lordship's masterly exposition of the unfavourable way in which the loss, through England's supineness, of the impalpable influence called prestige, has operated in inducing the Turcomans to carry their submission to the White Czar; and the further disasters which he foreshadowed from a persistence of such supineness, afford graphic illustration of the principle laid down in my Paper above referred to, as governing small States lying between two large ones—that, namely, of POLITICAL GRAVITATION. In obedience to this, as to a law of their political existence, small States so situated gravitate towards the Power which is, or seems to be in their circumscribed horizon, the larger and stronger. Lord Granville's strictures in the course of the controversy that Lord Salisbury's views were "entirely Oriental," would appear to ordinary understandings, judging by the "rule of square and the fitness of things," to point to a special qualification for the duty of judicious criticism of an Oriental subject dealing with Oriental races. But that it should be alleged by Lord Granville as a ground of disqualification against his adversary in this connection, makes us cease to wonder at his diplomatic discomfiture in respect of the annexation of Merv being sprung like a bomb under his feet, while endeavouring to cope with his exclusively European, although admittedly most able and polished modes of correspondence and official intercourse, with the quasi-Oriental Russian diplomatists. Their dispatches, throughout the Blue Book under review, are redolent with *gōl bāt*,—a term in Oriental diplomacy meaning, literally, a round phrase—exhibiting no salient points to be laid hold of, but revolving at the will of the author so as to present a new phase to each successive objection. Lord Granville deprecates the imputation that he "was the dupe of any representation about Merv." Far be it from me to insinuate anything so discourteous. It may be submitted, however, in view of his own admission to the House, "that he believed it was impossible that Russia would advance," whether the spirit of his negotiations was not instinct with too sublime a confidence, leading, on discovery of misplacement, to vain reproaches of bad faith, and unavailing

"Tears from the depth of some divine despair."

In presence of such unsophisticated simplicity and primitive innocence one is irresistibly led to ask, "Are we in Arcady? or in a wicked warring world?" Had there been no assurances of a similar character from the same quarter about Khiva but a short decade before? And should not the proved hollowness of those assurances, and the vast advance of Russia towards our North-West Frontier, from the 42° parallel of latitude to the 36° in the interval, have suggested caution?

Enough, perhaps, has been adduced on the testimony of published official documents to dispose of the claim advanced by the Foreign Office under its present *personnel* to the continued confidence of the nation for the conduct of the eminently delicate situation on the North-West Frontier of India, entailed through its past management.

I may venture to hope, then, that the way has been cleared for the submission of my humble views as recorded in my Papers above cited. The main policy which I have all along advocated is the concluding of an intimate alliance with Persia, offensive and defensive. The considerations on which I based that advocacy are set forth in the following extract, pp. 12, 13, 14.

"Now, the question as to whether Persia is the pioneer of Russia, long suspected and practically assumed by England in the wars waged for the maintenance of the integrity of Afghanistan as the outwork of India,—the said assumption, on the other hand, being scouted by Mr. Eastwick as 'preposterous,'—this vexed question I shall not stop here to consider, regarding it as beyond the scope of practical politics. On this head I would only remark that Persia, in her position between Russia and England, but illustrates, though on a slightly larger scale, the law of POLITICAL GRAVITATION enunciated in a previous part of this paper, and exemplified by the cases of

Eastern Turkistan and Afghanistan. If, then, Persia should have shown an apparent preferential leaning towards Russia, it would only imply that Russia's policy had been more vigorous and judicious than our own,—assuming the strength of the two Powers to be equal. With the Caspian converted into a Russian lake, and her columns pushing their way steadily across Central Asia, consolidating their power at each stage by the construction of a chain of forts, wells, depôts, etc., and England, on the other hand, pursuing only a policy 'of masterly inactivity,' what was Persia to do? Once let there be a change to a vigorous policy, calculated to reassure that Power that her true interest and safety point to a firm alliance with England, and we shall assuredly have no cause to complain of her preferential leaning to any other Power. The geographical position of Persia points her out as the natural ally of England in the East. Her seaboard adjoins our own, thus enabling the British fleet to afford protection in common to both countries, and to furnish supplies and succours to our ally if required at any conjuncture. Further, the steadfast alliance of Persia would enable us to prosecute under greater advantages, equally political as material, the project of railway communication between India and Europe *via* the Euphrates valley route; also to perfect our telegraph lines.

"British influence at the court of Teheran once firmly established on the solid and enduring basis of a conviction on both sides of mutual interest, the time would have arrived to furnish British Officers to organise and command a powerful contingent in Persia.* Prior to, or in the absence of, an alliance on such an assured basis, the renewal of the experiment which had failed before would again, I apprehend, be found premature and ineffectual. Such a policy, while securing our frontier in the north-west from actual attack for an indefinite period, practically for ever, would place our power and prestige in India on so firm and enduring a basis, reassuring our friends and hopelessly discouraging our enemies, that I believe we might largely reduce our European force with perfect safety, and carry on the work of educating and in other ways training the natives for the progressive filling of civil offices under the Government without any fear of a misconstruction of our motives.

"In anticipation of the adoption of the policy above sketched, it is assumed, of course, that concurrently with the appointment

---

* The Shah applied for this on his visit to England in 1873.

of a special political officer for the conduct of the duties of the north-west frontier in India, the British minister at Teheran shall have been selected with reference to his experience of Oriental courts and special qualifications, as proved by his success at the same.

"The last point that occurs to me as possible to be raised as a ground of objection to the policy in question has reference to the umbrage that may perhaps be taken by Russia. That policy being strictly of a defensive character, such an objection to it does not appear to me worthy to be considered. In former treaties with Persia it was provided, as Mr. Eastwick informs us, that that Power should prevent any invasion of India on the side of Afghanistan; and since at that early period Russia had made no progress in Central Asia, and consequently the treaties in question, as the exponents of a defensive policy, could not have been formed with any reference to Russia, the revival of such engagement with Persia at the present day cannot constitute any legitimate cause of umbrage to Russia. It only remains then for England to adopt such a policy as may be dictated by a regard to the national interests, irrespective of the view that may be taken of the same by any foreign power. That policy being, as above stated, strictly of a defensive character, should umbrage be taken at it by Russia it would only imply the entertainment on her part of ulterior aggressive views which this defensive policy was calculated to thwart. The sooner therefore that issue were joined on the question, while as yet Russia has attained no vantage ground in Central Asia to disturb us in India, and her plans for the renewal of her attempt in Turkey are not matured, so much the better for us. We are prepared for all contingencies. But since a preparedness for war is the best security for peace, it may safely be assumed that, in view of this attitude, issue will not be joined in the present day. That day—the *dies iracundiæ*—in all human calculation will practically be put off for ever by the effective barrier which the exhibition of a determined, steadfast policy may be expected to raise up on our North-western Frontier. Such a barrier once consolidated under a strong government, we might proceed with safety to economise our military expenditure in India, and in the remission of obnoxious taxes thereby facilitated, remove one serious bar to the contentment of the people under our rule."

Assuming that the advantage of a closer alliance with Persia on the basis indicated should have become apparent to England on weighing the above considerations, how is the correlative conviction of mutual interest to be impressed on the mind of the Shah? Premising that the gaining by the British Ambassador at Teheran of the absolute and entire confidence of the Shah is the one essential and indispensable prerequisite to any practical good in furtherance of British policy issuing from any such alliance, a consideration of the widely different modes of thought, feeling, and action obtaining between European and Oriental Courts would seem *prima facie* to have implied the appointment to Teheran of an officer trained in the diplomacy of the latter. And history, by its examples, recalls the precedents established in the days when the foundations of our Indian Empire were firmly laid, and the superstructure successfully reared thereon to its present stately proportions. In 1808, when Napoleon contemplated the conquest of India, and, in conjunction with Alexander of Russia, had planned to march an army through Persia and Afghanistan, supported by a movement in Southern India headed by French officers, Sir John Malcolm was accredited to the Court of Persia, and weaning the Shah from the Franco-Russian alliance, frustrated the plan. Again, Mountstuart Elphinstone, a little later, was deputed to the Court of the Ameer of Afghanistan on a similar defensive mission, and was equally successful. Again, at later stages of our defensive political combinations, rendered necessary by Russia's persistent advance, Sir Justin Shiel, Sir John McNeil, and Sir Henry Rawlinson, all experienced Oriental diplomatists, were successively accredited to the Court of Persia. Of late, however—and these the critical years during which Russia has been suffered to push her columns eastward from the Caspian unobstructed, albeit along a line conterminous with the Persian border—the presumption is irresistible that the British relations at Teheran have been in the hands of a diplomatist who, however generally able as the chosen representative of the English Foreign Office, nevertheless lacked the indispensable qualification of Eastern training and experience necessary to enable him to acquire the personal confidence of the Shah, and thus attain a commanding influence in the councils of his Court. The adverse presumptions against Mr. Thomson's suitability for the post in question culminate to conclusive proof in view of his last dispatch recorded in the Central Asia Blue Book above quoted, wherein, on the 10th February last (1884), replying to Lord Granville, he telegraphs, "I have no confirmation of reported submission of Merv chiefs. Intelligence just received, dated the 3rd February, states that chiefs had rejected Russian demand for submission," &c. Mr. Thomson's blindness to the important events passing under his very eyes affords a notable illustration of the Oriental proverb: "There is darkness under the lamp!"

It does not appear from the correspondence that Mr., now Sir Ronald Thomson, ever proceeded in person to the Russo-Persian Frontier, even when the critical negotiations regarding the basis of the delimitation of boundary were in progress.

I venture to affirm that there is not a single Indian official within the three Presidencies who, if placed in that post, would not have considered it his first duty to march to the frontier, and there pitching his tent insist on representing England in the Delimitation Commission, and would only have struck it after carrying his point, or, if unsupported by the Foreign Office, resigning his appointment in practical protest.

We cease to wonder, then, that Sir Ronald Thomson's answers to his official chief's enquiries, from first to last throughout that eventful period, were such, through want of accurate information, as entirely to mislead him.

Assuming then that a suitable appointment to the Teheran Embassy will be arranged by Sir Ronald Thomson's promotion to a more appropriate European post, the Ambassador selected as his successor would have much leeway to bring up. Since the year 1869, the date of my Paper, proposing the intimate alliance in question with Persia, and the arranging of a neutral zone in pursuance of Lord Clarendon's plan, how much has not been lost and gained in the interval by the rival parties! No neutral zone is now possible, the respective boundaries of Russia and Afghanistan having become conterminous. Our hand is forced by Russia's advance to strategic points within the territorial scope of the arranged delimitation commission. Immediate action is demanded. Paramount considerations of national policy demand that it shall be of the most decided and uncompromising vigour, regardless of cost. On this latter point indeed it is but a question of comparative cost, looking to the ultimate issue, in respect to which any outlay, however large, entailed by present defensive arrangements would, I venture to predict, be found the truest economy.

The steps in our countermove necessitated by Russia's "unprovoked aggression" on our ally, Ameer Abdulrahman's territory, are:—

1. To demand the withdrawal of her troops to the Sarakhs parallel. In the probable contingency of her paying no heed to that demand, under present circumstances the British Am-

bassador at St. Petersburg to be withdrawn. This would be strictly in accordance with the course laid down by De Vattel, Book III., Chap. IV., to meet the proceeding adopted by Russia in the present case, and which may be described in the subjoined words of that authority.* Such decided indication of our determination to support the Ameer in defending the integrity of Afghan territory, coupled with Lord Granville's complaint of Russia's bad faith in the seizure of Merv in his speech on the 11th of March, 1884, debate—and which should now be utilized as a formal protest against that measure—may be left to ferment as yeast in the discontented hearts of the Turkomans at their subjugation. Fortunately Russia's practical renunciation of the Lumsden Commission has saved us from the condonation of the annexation of Merv, which otherwise the impolitic negotiations with Russia about that Commission would *pro tanto* have constituted. It is not every blunder that has such a fortunate issue.

2. To move the Shah to enter a formal protest to the Russian Government against the annexation of Merv in violation of his legitimate territorial claim to the oasis on the Murghâb—although long lying dormant, and his Tekke subjects of the territory in question being often in open and successful resistance to his authority. Persia has never ignored their allegiance, nor abandoned her claim

---

* "To march an army into a neighbouring country by which we are not threatened, and without having endeavoured to obtain by reason and justice an equitable reparation of the wrongs of which we complain, would be introducing a mode pregnant with evils to mankind, and sapping the foundations of the safety and tranquility of States. If this mode of proceeding be not exploded and proscribed by the public indignation and the concurrence of every civilized people, it will become necessary to continue always in a military posture and to keep ourselves constantly on our guard, no less in times of profound peace than during the existence of declared and open war."

to the territory. Mr. Thomson in his despatch dated February 13th, 1882 (No. 20 of the B.B. of 1884), while reporting that "in view of the cost and risk the Persian Government had decided that they could not attempt an armed occupation of their territory," adds, "They had therefore determined to abstain" *for the present* (the italics are mine), "from all interference with Merv and the Tejjen districts occupied by Tekke Turkomans, and instructions in this sense had been sent to the Prince-Governor of Khorassan for the guidance of the local authorities in that province." Persia therefore would be strictly within her *de jure* rights in making such a protest. Its proclamation far and wide throughout the Turkoman districts, would encourage the large portion of the tribes who are opposed to the annexation, and legitimatize their efforts to regain their national independence. It will here be seen that Persia's supremacy over them was little more than nominal, and therefore more congenial than the centralized rule of a strong power like Russia. The official information published in *The Times* telegram of 29th March last that a hostile encounter ensued between the Russian force sent at the end of February preceding to occupy Merv and some of the Turkomans, and that thereafter a great number of families went forth, self-expatriated from the annexed territory, is significant.

3. Furnishing British Officers to drill and command Persian levies, in late retrieval of the blindness of the Government of the day in rejecting such application when made by the Shah during his visit to England in 1873. One or more specially selected officers to be stationed at Sarakhs, to give effect to an invitation by the Shah to his Turkoman subjects to enrol themselves for military service

under the Persian flag, by offers of good pay and congenial privileges. The success which has attended our efforts in this direction in India in reclaiming the Bheels, Meenas, and other equally wild tribes with the Turkomans, and converting them into faithful disciplined soldiers, warrants a reasonable hope that similar efforts would not be without good effect in that field also.

4. The Island of Karack, in the Persian Gulf, to be fortified and converted into an impregnable *place d'armes* as a base and depôt for munitions of war, in support of military operations that may be found necessary in Persia, to flank the Russian advance on Herat. Convicts from the Andamans might be temporarily brought round for the economical construction of the works. The commodious natural harbour formed by the sheltered anchorage between the Islands of Karack and Cargo, with a depth of water ranging from six to sixteen fathoms, would accommodate the largest fleet that England might find it necessary to station in the Persian Gulf.

5. Construct a railroad from the Gulf to Teheran, and on to Meshed, with branches to Sarakhs and Herat. All important at the present day as a strategic line, it would eventually form a connecting link in our overland communication between India and England, viâ the Euphrates Valley.

Concurrently with the above measures to flank the Russian advance on Herat on the west (on the side of Persia) and to raise the Turkoman tribes in her rear, the measures to be taken in Afghanistan would have to be of the most energetic and comprehensive character. The Government would appear to have been at length awakened by the annexation of Merv, from its dream of blissful reliance on Russia's professions and protestations in regard to the end and aim of her Central Asian operations, by the orders issued for the construction of the railway to Quetta. This work will have to be done thoroughly, not halting at Quetta, but pushed on to Candahar. Herat to be fortified by British Engineers, supported by a small auxiliary British force.

The foregoing measures may suffice to place our Northwest Frontier defences in as satisfactory a position as would seem practicable at this late day. The decided attitude evinced will probably avail to secure compliance with our reasonable demands on behalf of our allies. If otherwise, however, and her posts are attacked, the situation will be retrieved not by the modern euphemism of "carrying on military operations," but in the good old English fashion of a declaration of war, which Russia and the world will understand means the putting forth of the whole resources of the British and Greater England's Empire for the defence of that Empire.

"We can govern India, we cannot govern Egypt." Why? Because we have at the head of the Government a minister who, in disregard of England's ancient policy of cultivating a cordial alliance with the Sultan of Turkey—the Caliph at once of our Indian Mahomedan, and Persia's Turcoman, subjects—stands committed to a sentimental denunciation of that Potentate, in his memorable and ever regrettable declaration in advocacy of the "Bag and Baggage" policy. At the period of the negotiations at Constantinople in 1882, resulting in the issue of the Identic Note by the Powers, I considered it my duty to submit for the consideration of the Foreign Office, my view of the situation, in despatches dated in margin,* in order to avert our direct armed intervention in Egypt, then impending, and the proposal of an alternative course calculated, in my humble judgment, to secure all legitimate objects of direct intervention divested of the risk of exciting the jealousy of the other European Powers. The course in question may be briefly described as proceeding in Egypt on our Indian system of working in the name of its legitimate suzerain, the Sultan, through a British Resident accredited to His Highness' appointed Viceroy. Since "*Delenda est,*" on the contrary, was the cry, and "military operations" was the peaceful device adopted, peace was waged with commendable vigour and varying fortune in that arduous field,— the historic memories of four thousand years looking down from the pyramids the while with a sad and eloquently silent wonderment at such fantastic freaks. After the lapse of nearly two years, public opinion in England, admonished by experience abroad and an increase to the Income Tax at home, suddenly woke up to a lively sense of the situation, and piteously asked through its accredited organ*: " Why can't we govern Egypt on the Indian protected State system, in the masterful grasp of a British Resident?" [Q. E. D.]

To Earl Granville, dated 20th July, 1882.
To Earl Granville, dated 26th July, 1882.
From Lord Tinterden, dated Aug. 1, 1882; (acknowledging receipt.)

Further, it is satisfactory to me to have had my humble view of how we should deal with Egypt confirmed by the high authority of the greatest statesman in Europe. In his speech in the Reichstag on the 2nd instant, Prince Bismarck stated "that he had on several occasions been asked his advice, on behalf of the British Government, as to how they should deal with Egypt, both by his personal and political friend, the late Lord Ampthill, acting under

---

* *Times,* 24th June, 1884.

instructions from his Government, and also through the medium of their own representatives in England. Now, to those inquiries I always replied if I were an English Minister I would seek the mediation of the Sultan, in order through him, to obtain a position in Egypt, by means of which English interests would be safeguarded. I also said I was of the opinion that this method of procedure would not be likely to give offence to other nations . . . ." Precisely the view, and almost identical in terms, it will be observed, with that which I submitted for the consideration of the Government in July, 1882.

Great misapprehension has arisen, unfortunately, both in England and in our Colonies, in regard to the motives which have actuated Prince Bismarck in his recent encouragement of Colonial aspirations on the part of Germany. Aggressive views have been attributed to him, which a little reflection on the changed conditions with which he has had to deal in the expansion of the Kingdom of Prussia into the German Empire, might have shown to be groundless. While as yet Prussia was isolated and comparatively landlocked there was no scope for Colonial enterprise. But with the incorporation of the Hanseatic towns and commercial seaports, such as Hamburg, Bremen, Lubec, &c., the trading communities of the same naturally demanded fresh fields for their expanding commerce. Not only, however, is there nothing of an aggressive character in the Prince's measures for supplying such natural wants, but it is manifest that, in view of Germany's status as a maritime Power, every fresh colony planted out is, as it were, giving an additional pledge to fortune, and therefore, to peace. It would seem important that this non-aggressive aspect of recent German Colonial enterprises should be rightly understood, both here to modify public opinion, and more particularly in our Colonies, on whose loyal co-operation and aid England relies on being confronted with a really aggressive Power like that of Russia.

A word at parting to the Coming Two Millions:—

My Fellow Countrymen,—You have been called to take part in the solemn and responsible duty of governing your country. Not a day too soon. For the ancient constituencies, whose votes you are called upon to supplement, have been deluded by the plausible professions of one eloquent orator into electing for the most part dummies, chained to his chariot wheels. Hence has arisen the pernicious influence on Parliamentary proceedings of the ONE-MAN POWER —dominating the House and overriding all healthy discussion on the most vital national questions. And the several associated "interests," Railway, Shipping, and others, into which the Commons are banded in class cliques, are well content to have it so. For each finds in the packed, obedient majority at the Prime Minister's back and beck a convenient instrument for the promotion of his peculiar class legislation. And so it has come about that while the people are starving during this universal trade depression for want of work, the sordid money-making middle-class are enabled to maintain their class legislation for free imports of manufactured goods, by means of which the English capitalist, who sends his capital abroad to employ cheap foreign labour, is enabled to bring in his goods so produced, and undersell the home manufacturer in the English market. The large consuming class being thus pauperised, the agriculturist loses his natural customers at his door. If the workman, without work or wages, complains and asks for bread, he is told that bread is cheapened under the system of free imports, and is given a stone in the shape of a Board of Trade Return, showing that the total wealth of the nation has increased. What boots it to the working man at the bottom of the scale if the total wealth of the country has increased, through accretions at the top, unless it filtrates down to his level? It is sheer mockery! No. We must level up, and if in the process, the respectable middle-class MONEY BAGS should find the tables turned by advanced legislation in the future, he will only have himself to thank for being wholly absorbed selfishly in money-making, regardless of the means or instruments, or of injury inflicted on whole classes of his toiling countrymen.

"*Rem, honeste si possis, sed quocumque modo, Rem.*"

That's his motto. The daily published acknowledgments by the Chancellor of the Exchequer of sums received as conscience-money from A. B. C. and X. Y. Z., and every conceivable combination of the intermediate letters of the alphabet, is significant. It is to be hoped that when the initials are handed up by the "Accusing Spirit" to Heaven's Chancery, the "Recording Angel" will be able to identify them, and thus to drop the absolving tear upon their false returns and blot them out for ever. Otherwise their late repentance and the alarming sacrifice at which it was sought to be consummated, would, alas! be all in vain.

I daresay you have all heard of the population of England being likened to a pot of beer—froth at the top, dregs at the bottom, good sound liquor in the middle. Depend upon it, my countrymen, that simile sprung from the kindred inspiration as the picture of the fight between the lion and the man, painted by the man. "Ah," said the king of beasts, contemplating the work, "if a lion had painted that picture, the man would have been underneath and the lion at top!" I leave my readers to draw the moral.

I have passed my life on foreign service in India, and am thus a stranger to you. It is therefore but a proper mark of respect when aspiring to the honour of addressing a body of my countrymen to explain, in conclusion, the ground on which I venture to think I may be permitted do so without the charge of presumption—especially on a question connected with India.

In now bidding you farewell, I would only hope that if the views of foreign policy and domestic legislation which I have ventured to submit for your consideration shall meet with your approval, you will exercise the powers conferred upon you ",without partiality, favour, or affection," in returning fit members to Parliament, so as to strengthen the hands of our beloved Sovereign in affording the choice of capable Ministers. As Queen of England, Her Majesty has ever shown her sympathetic and disinterested interest in all her subjects. As Empress of India she can have but one sole individual concern in the maintenance of our splendid Empire in the East, and in the protection and welfare of its loyal Princes and people.

Printed by Libri Plureos GmbH in Hamburg, Germany